A GIFT OF
CHRISTMAS JOY
for

Craig

MANNHEIM STEAMROLLER

Christmas

THE
Season
FOR *Joy*

By Chip Davis

Thomas Nelson
Since 1798

NASHVILLE   DALLAS   MEXICO CITY   RIO DE JANEIRO   BEIJING

Published in Nashville, TN, by Thomas Nelson. Thomas Nelson is a trademark of Thomas Nelson, Inc.

Thomas Nelson, Inc., titles may be purchased in bulk for educational, business, fundraising, or sales promotional use. For information, please email SpecialMarkets@ThomasNelson.com.

All scripture references are from the New King James Version of the Bible (NKJV)
©1979, 1980, 1982, 1992, Thomas Nelson, Inc., Publisher. Used by permission. All rights reserved.

Designed by ThinkPen Design, LLC | Springdale, Arkansas

ISBN–10: 1–4041–0511–5
ISBN–13: 978–14041–0511-9

Printed in the United States of America

TABLE *of* CONTENTS

5

The Season of Joy

The Christmas season is one of incredible joy. Our holiday traditions remind us of warm family memories, while the excitement of our children brings fresh wonder to this ancient festival.

Christmas is a full-being experience. Our spirits celebrate with the joy of the holiday season, while our senses take us on a journey through past, present, and future. We sing, dance to, or even simply listen to music both ancient and new. We feast on traditional family recipes and tell our little ones about enjoying Christmas meals at our grandmother's house. The smells of evergreen boughs and fresh pies guide us through countless memories, while the sights of the season offer a panorama of traditional and contemporary festive décor.

Experiencing Christmas fully means embracing all that is good in it—most of all celebrating the Child who is at the heart of season and the source of true joy.

My hope for you this Christmas is that you savor the season of joy.

Chip

Joy of Wonder

Star of wonder, star of night!
Star of royal beauty bright;
Westward leading, still proceeding,
Guide us to thy Perfect Light.

JOHN HENRY HOPKINS

SAVOR THE WONDER

*W*hy is Christmas different than any other time of the year? Why is the season so alive and vibrant?

Our hearts beat just a little bit differently around Christmas and the reason can be summed up in one word: wonder.

Christmas gives adults permission to be children again. And what do we do when we are children again? Our grownup defenses come down. We laugh and play with friends. We let go of grievances and forgive more easily. We visit a simple manger scene at the church down the street and don't see neighbors in bathrobes, but the shepherds of two thousand years ago. As life goes on, many things become more complicated until we're stripped of our sense of mystery and can no longer see the wonders of love and faith right before our eyes. To be able to experience that wonder again is one of the best parts of Christmas—but it's only available when we see with the eyes of a child!

One of my most vivid childhood memories of Christmas was during a candlelight Christmas Eve service when I went out the back stairs of the church, still in my choir robe, to listen for Santa's sleigh. It was a chilly night with beautiful moonlight. My mom and dad had helped wrap fresh evergreen boughs that adorned the railings of the church—and they smelled so fresh and alive. The evergreen scent was complimented by wood smoke rising from fireplaces all over our small town in northwest Ohio.

The night was crystal clear. The stars twinkled. And I could swear that I heard Santa coming. It was an unforgettable night that made an indelible impression on me as a child. It was a night made for wonder, and that night has never left me.

I hope I never grow up and miss the wonder of Christmas. I hope that a Baby wrapped in swaddling clothes and all the other sights and sounds of the season continue to strike a chord in my heart like I felt that Christmas Eve so many years ago.

Twinkle, twinkle, little star
How I **wonder** *. . .*

KEEP WONDERING

*I*t's so important to keep the wonder, especially during the holiday season. The things we do—like taking a little child outside to look up at the stars and maybe listen for the sound of angels' wings as they come again to announce a birth—are so meaningful. And when I see wonder in the faces of my kids, you better believe it creeps and then joyfully explodes on my face as well. It's inescapable. It's one of the ways I rekindle that wonder and joy inside myself, by seeing my kids captured by beautiful possibilities.

If you want to create wondrous experiences for your family, start by looking inside for something simple or a memory from your childhood. Scent, sound, and taste especially evoke those magical times and bring back those memories.

Creating memories doesn't always come easy. It can take a lot of planning and work to discover and share the feelings you want. But even work, when done to bless others, has a wonder of its own.

If you want to experience more joy and wonder for the season—but are feeling a little bit like Scrooge—start simple by giving something from your heart to those you love. If your cookies are store bought—make them yourself this year. If you are a horrible artist—draw pictures for your kids' rooms anyway. If you can't sing—you can still deliver the sound of joy as you take the whole family caroling in the neighborhood.

Why not throw your heart into creating something that you can bring out at Christmas every year. Homemade ornaments; a small crèche for the front yard; a reindeer light display that will be the envy of your neighbors?

But don't work alone. Like the slogan says: Let's build something together. Good or bad, whatever you craft will not compare to the memory created.

This will bring joy to you—and those you love. It will stick with them for a long time after you are gone. Those are the kind of things that have a lot of deep worth in them.

Joy isn't found in getting a thing; it's in creating a memory.

Memories are like starlight: they go on forever.

BILL FRIES (AS C. W. MCCALL)

"SLOW AS CHRISTMAS"

There's a song in the air. There's a Star in the sky. Music is all around us in nature. Last night I heard an interesting bird that I hadn't heard before, and my son, who's a really good whistler, managed to talk to him. He got that bird to fly across the ravine and sit in a nearby tree. My son listened carefully, learned the new song, and shared in the music.

I need that in my life. May I encourage you this season to have an open and listening mind? To pay attention to all that God has created around you, both the people you see and the beauty of His world? (I wonder how many people passed by a lowly manger two thousand years ago and never even suspected that the world was about to change.)

A lot of gifts are given to us constantly, but we often miss them because we don't recognize them in the forms of new birds and tasty little plums and starry nights. Slow down. Wonder isn't the gift of just one moment; it's the culmination of many moments. "Slow as Christmas" should be a phrase about savoring time, not lamenting its crawl.

Take time to enjoy the gifts of the natural world. Watch a sunset. That's a simple one. Just watch as the sun goes down and the colors change. This amazing event happens every evening, even during the extra-busy Christmas season—you just have to get outside a couple hours earlier than summer. Notice the lowness of the light as it casts long shadows. When the sun gets down to the top of the horizon it lights up the bottom of the trees and everything else goes into shadows. It's like there's a big, orange spotlight coming from the sky.

Slowing down to pay attention to little things fuels the fire of wonder—and brings a quiet joy to our soul.

Rise, happy morn, rise, holy morn,
Draw forth the cheerful day from night:
O Father, touch the East, and light
The light that shone when Hope was born.

ALFRED, LORD TENNYSON

Joy of Family

For unto us a Child is born,
Unto us a Son is given;
And the government will be upon His shoulder.
And His name will be called
Wonderful, Counselor, Mighty God,
Everlasting Father, Prince of Peace.

ISAIAH 9:6

FAMILY FIRST

The best way to make Christmas especially meaningful for your family is to put your family first . . . all year long.

Love them well. They're the most important people to you on earth, and the care you invest in them will produce returns far beyond your lifetime.

Enjoy time with them. You will never simply have time for them; you must make time for them and make the most of it.

Appreciate them. The people in your family—with all their quirks and charms—are precious gifts. Don't take them for granted. Remember to say "thank you" for them and to them as you reflect on what each person means to you.

Celebrate with them. Christmas is the
perfect season to forgive each other for being
human, rebuild bridges, enjoy the good
things you have in common, and celebrate
something far bigger than yourself—the family of
all mankind.

On that first Christmas night, angels announced, "Peace on
earth!" What better place can that begin than in your family?

Today's Christmas should mean
creating happy hours for tomorrow
and reliving those of yesterday.

GLADYS TABER

"CHRISTMAS LULLABY"
KELLY'S SONG

*I*t's true: Children grow up far too quickly. (And sometimes it feels like we grow old too quickly!)

But with some thoughtful effort you can create Christmas traditions with them that will help them relive their joyful memories even when they have families of their own. The important things are to make it special, do it together, and keep it fresh every year.

When my daughter Kelly was four years old, I wanted to do something special for her, so I made up a story about Santa going home to the North Pole on Christmas night for dinner with Mrs. Claus. And, if we were out in the yard at the right time we might hear him.

The engineers at my recording studio made a continuous loop of sleigh bells that would fade up and fade down, and I put it in the barn in a boom box, just faint enough to be believable. This adventure also required binoculars and a compass we called our "Santa finder."

Together Kelly and I would try to figure out where Santa was in the night sky.

In one of those moments you can't plan, some little private jet was screaming south to north, and Kelly started yelling, "Santa, we're down here. We're down here!" It was incredible—the timing of that—the sleigh bells came on, and the jet went streaming across the sky. We knew that was Santa.

No other year could quite match the drama of that Gulf Stream streaking across the sky, but you can believe that Kelly and I never missed our annual night watch together—even though she is all grown up now.

After that first Christmas searching for Santa with Kelly, I wrote a lullaby for her. Seeing her peaceful little four-year-old face snuggled up with the blankets and the pillow—that to me was a picture of Christmas joy.

Maybe your time with a son or daughter will never turn into a lullaby, but I'll bet you get exactly what you and yours need to celebrate a lifetime of love.

"CATCHING SNOWFLAKES ON YOUR TONGUE"
EVAN'S SONG

Great memories are made up of little moments. Treasure those times. Learn to see the joy in every day, and you'll find Christmas all year long.

The song I wrote for my son, Evan, was inspired by a winter moment that happened when he was four years old. My wife, Trisha, was outside with Evan teaching him how to catch snowflakes on his tongue. The snowstorm was just beginning to pour its biggest, fluffiest snowflakes onto the earth, and my loved ones happily ran around the yard to catch as many as they could. When their feet got cold, they ran into the house and sat in front of the fireplace, propping their socked feet in front of the flame. But Evan was too excited to sit still. He didn't even wait to put his shoes back on before rushing back outside to catch more snowflakes.

The song inspired by this event is
one of our favorites in the Mannheim
Steamroller family, and it's on the CD in
this book. Every time I hear it, I can still see
my wife and son running around outside
under the white sky of the snowstorm, Evan's
blonde hair bouncing. It was one of those
classic moments—a snowy afternoon, a child's
excitement, and a fire in the fireplace—exactly the kind of family
memory that makes Christmas a time of wonder and joy.

The heart is like a treasure chest
that's filled with souvenirs;
it's where we keep the memories
we've gathered through the years.

ANONYMOUS

"FELIZ NAVIDAD"
ELYSE'S SONG

*E*ven the uncomfortable misunderstandings of life—especially those within the safety of a loving family—can be overcome with gentle humor and encouragement. Learning to laugh at yourself is a tremendous gift both for you and for your family. Life's too important to take everything too seriously. Let joy reign all year long.

A few years ago, my family came to visit me in San Antonio while I was on tour. As a special treat, someone helped me rent a river boat and arrange to have dinner catered there for my family and a few of the Steamroller people who travel with us, and to make the evening even more special, he hired a thirteen-piece mariachi band to play during dinner. When that band spooled up—man, it was rocking. (I was especially grateful for this because, knowing my son and how active he is, I knew that if he got bored, he probably could have turned that simple boat ride into a whitewater rafting trip.)

About halfway through the trip, the band started playing "Feliz Navidad,"

and my younger daughter, Elyse, got a funny look on her face. Her older sister, Kelly, was just enjoying the music, and Evan was entertained enough not to try to jump into the water, but Elyse didn't seem to be enjoying herself. The longer the song went on, the more uncomfortable she looked. Then the band started playing closer and closer to her, and the more they did that, the more she withdrew. Pretty soon she was in Mommy's lap, and when the band stepped even closer, Elyse went under the table. Later we found out that she thought they were singing "Elyse Navidad" and were making fun of her.

If you knew her now, how she can laugh at just about anything, especially herself, you would smile at the memory of the indignant frown she threw at that mariachi band. She laughs about it now, of course, just as the rest of us do. Family memories have a way of doing that, of drawing us together and giving us fuel for laughter for years to come. And at Christmastime, we have a unique opportunity to laugh with those we love as we remember those past Christmases.

It is good to be children sometimes, and never better than at Christmas, when its mighty Founder was a child Himself.

CHARLES DICKENS

"HAVE YOURSELF A MERRY LITTLE CHRISTMAS"
TRISHA'S SONG

*C*hildren are wonderful, and it's easy to pour all your love and creative energy into them. But your spouse is more than just your co-pilot in getting through life. At Christmastime, you've got to make life merry for this brave, amazing person who's entrusted you with his or her heart and future.

Usually on Christmas night, after we've done all our traditions and put away the Santa finders and the kids are all crashed out, my wife and I sit on the couch with a glass of red wine and watch the fire glowing in the fireplace. It's a romantic end to the wonderful day behind us: Mommy Claus and Daddy Claus just relaxing and reflecting on the things that happened in the course of Christmas Day. We murmur things like, "Did you see them when they opened . . . ? Did you see her face when . . . ?" The conversation allows us to savor the joy a little bit more, to stretch it out a little bit longer into the evening hours.

These quiet, sweet moments with Trisha inspired me to arrange "Have Yourself a Merry Little Christmas" as a gift for her and our family. The slow, almost swing beat reminds me of dancing in the

living room and all the beautiful Christmases we've shared together.
Whether writing a song or just writing a note in a beautiful card, we all need to find ways to express our love and appreciation for the people closest to us. Each of them is a precious gift.

The Christian is supposed to love
his neighbor, and since his wife
is his nearest neighbor, she
should be his deepest love.

MARTIN LUTHER

Joy of Giving

Somehow not only for Christmas
But all the year through,
The joy that you give to others
Is the joy that comes back to you.
And the more you spend in blessing
The poor and lonely and sad,
The more of your heart's possessing
Returns to make you glad.

JOHN GREELEAF WHITTIER

GIVE YOURSELF

Y̶ou give your family something more important, more perfect than anything you could buy from a store when you give of yourself. If you're good at cooking, make them a meal. If you're good at building things, construct a playhouse or camp-out cabin. You might think you're only good at handling business or doing mundane, everyday tasks, but that just means you really need Christmas to remind you of the many diverse gifts that have been placed in you.

Try making Christmas ornaments for your family, even if all you do is fill a glass ball with slips of paper listing things you love about them. Put a photo of your family in a picture frame along with a caption that reads "Top Priority," and set it on your desk; then show your kids that you have this daily reminder to help you stay on track and put loving them well at the top of your list. Make "dates" with each of your children and have special one-on-one outings. These are irreplaceable gifts—they're gifts of yourself.

I have a talent for music. My parents and grandparents nurtured this gift from my earliest childhood, and now I make a living by sharing this blessing. But no matter how busy I become—whether making music for Mannheim fans or developing ambience-enhanced pain-management therapies for hospitals—I always make sure my family gets the best of my efforts. They hear my best music; they receive the most of my time. It's sometimes hard. It takes discipline and practice and sacrifice. But it's worth it!

On my newest Christmas album I've included songs for each person in my immediate family, songs that celebrate colorful moments in our lives, as a gesture of what they mean to me.

Whatever gifts you have, use them to create and celebrate memories of love and joy in your family.

The ordinary acts we practice every day
at home are of more importance to the soul
than their simplicity might suggest.

THOMAS MOORE

MY FATHER'S GIFT TO ME

You've discovered by now that I love to give wonderful gifts to my children. Nothing brings me joy like bringing them joy. But even if I spend a lifetime thinking of ways to enchant them, I don't think I can ever equal in giving what my father did for me. He was the high school choir instructor and led music in our church choir, so we weren't a wealthy family. Rich; yes. Wealthy; no. But his gift had nothing to do with money.

Growing up in the 60s, if I'd been like other teens, my highest aspirations would have centered on starting a rock and roll band and being part of the next super group. Instead, I loved classical music—and since my dad played a mean jazz sax, yes, I loved classic Glenn Miller style jazz.

I once told my dad that I would love to hear a particular classical piece on the instrument it was written for, which was the harpsichord. If you haven't noticed, there aren't a lot of harpsichords for sale at the mall—or even on eBay.

Do you realize how much my life changed . . . can you imagine how loved I felt . . . when a year later I got my wish? I did get to hear—and even play—that piece on the harpsichord.

My dad wrote letters and went to the library until he could find the plans to make a harpsichord. He built it for me in his shop, and it still stands at my home as an expression of my father's love for me—and the greatest gift I ever received.

Christmas is love in action.
Every time we love,
every time we give,
it's Christmas.

DALE EVANS ROGERS

It is Christmas every time you let
God love others through you . . .
every time you smile at your brother
and offer him your hand.

MOTHER TERESA

The magi, as you know, were wise men—
wonderfully wise men who brought gifts
to the Babe in the manger. They invented
the art of giving Christmas presents.

O. HENRY

What can I give Him,
Poor as I am?
If I were a shepherd,
I would bring a lamb,
If I were a Wise Man
I would do my part—
Yet what I can I give him,
Give my heart.

CHRISTINA ROSSETTI

Miss no opportunity to do good.

JOHN WESLE

36

Joy of Music

Joy to the world, the Lord is come
Let earth receive her King
Let ev'ry heart prepare Him room
And heav'n and nature sing

Isaac Watts

MUSICAL HERITAGE

*A*t no time of the year do we experience a greater array of music than at Christmas. Speakers in every public building sing out everything from ancient carols to modern arrangements, and we've learned to love this splendid selection of holiday cheer. Christmas music is a beautiful part of our culture, inherited through generation after generation of people who love Christmas. It's part of who we are.

Music runs especially strong in my personal heritage. My grandmother was a piano teacher and the Methodist choir director who taught me music when I was little. My grandfather was a country doctor who also played the fiddle. He did a lot to encourage everybody to go into music. Both of my parents graduated from the University of Michigan music school. Music is part of who I am.

But whether your family nurtured you musically or whether your individual tastes came mainly through other influences, the songs of the Christmas season can create a bridge between you and every other person who honors the holiday time. This common heritage is a joy worth celebrating.

Music is well said to be the speech of angels; in fact, nothing among the utterances allowed to man is felt to be so divine. It brings us near to the infinite.

THOMAS CARLYLE

SURRISES

One of the joys of music is how it—like life—can surprise you. You might think a song will take you in one direction, but then the bridge spins you around and takes you down a completely different road.

Music has certainly found many ways to surprise me. When I was starting out in my early twenties I was adamant that I'd never live in Nebraska or write country music—and I ended up doing both. One of the commercial jingles that I helped write for an Omaha company became so popular that my partner and I—writing together as C. W. McCall—eventually had a number one country hit called "Old Home Filler Up and Keep On Truckin' Café," which led to "Wolf Creek Pass," which led to "Convoy," which sold 10 million copies and led to a movie of the same name. We had thirteen country hits in a row. To me, this was a freak sequence of events, one that changed my life.

To get to doing what I really love—the music of Mannheim Steamroller—I had to stretch and grow through other genres. I had to experience different things that, although they weren't where my heart was, gave me the chance to develop the discipline and contacts that would help me achieve my heart's desire, which was to be a composer. I didn't know that writing jingles would get me where I wanted to be, but it did.

A predictable life—like predictable music—is dull. Learn to make the most of your surprises, especially at Christmastime, when the pressure to create the perfect holiday experience so often overwhelms the joy of the season. Relax! Whether the holiday meets your expectations or surprises you with the unexpected, it's going to be wonder-full.

May you have the gladness of Christmas which is hope;
the spirit of Christmas which is peace;
the heart of Christmas which is love.

ADA V. HENDRICKS

JUST LISTEN

*A*t Christmas, when you feel overwhelmed by the busyness and maybe even depressed by the crush of obligations, please stop and take a cue from holiday music: The peppy tunes are mixed in with the more mellow, thoughtful ones. Let the music give you permission to enjoy the upbeat times while also insisting on some quiet moments. Remember, this is the season for both peace and goodwill. Let peace reign in your heart.

Peace is our gift to each other.

Elie Wiesel

STILLE NACHT
(SILENT NIGHT)

L. JOSEPH MOHR & M. FRANZ GRUBER, CIRCA 1818
TR. JOHN F. YOUNG, 1863

Tradition says this beloved carol was born in a
small German village shortly before Christmas.
The church's organ had broken, and the vicar, Joseph
Mohr, wrote this song as a way to celebrate the
season a cappella. This song showed up on our first
Christmas album, and it's still one of my favorites.

MUSICAL MEMORIES

Music is intimately connected with many of our most vivid memories. Lullabies evoke thoughts both of our mothers and of our own children when they were small. Something on the radio may remind us of our high school days, while other songs make us think of weddings or our grandmother's church or a loved one's funeral. That's part of the joy of music: We hear something and then see innumerable scenes unfold to its melody in our minds. The songs that touch our hearts that way are among the ones we love the most throughout our lives.

"Silent Night" is one of my favorite songs because it evokes powerful memories of my father. Many years ago during our first Christmas tour, when my dad was traveling with us as the piano technician, I remember playing the bells on "Stille Nacht" and seeing my dad sitting in the wings with the stage hands. They were all really moved by this highly nostalgic piece, and I was touched by their visible emotion. For years when we played that song, I couldn't keep back the tears as I relived that moment. And even now, every time I hear the strains of "Silent Night," I can still picture Dad sitting there off stage right.

This is the kind of memory that makes Christmas music so special. The songs carry us to other times. We may recall singing carols together as a family, or we might envision what it will be like when we share these musical treasures with our children and grandchildren. Whenever we hear the familiar refrains, we find ourselves at the intersection of our fondest dreams.

When Christmas bells are singing above the fields of snow,
we hear sweet voices ringing from lands of long ago,
and etched on vacant places are half-forgotten faces
of friends we used to cherish, and loves we used to know.

ELLA WHEELER WILCOX

Joy of Friends

*Friends are an indispensable part
of a meaningful life. They are
the ones who share our burdens
and multiply our blessings.*

BEVERLY LAHAYE

OLD FRIENDS

*F*ew joys in life can compare to the companionship of old and dear friends. When you've experienced mountains and valleys together, when you know each others' strengths and weaknesses and continue to love each other—that's gold!

One of the joys in my life is working with the people of Mannheim Steamroller and American Gramaphone. Over the decades, we've become much more than just business partners; we're truly friends. Who are the true friends in your life? Are they people you know from school? Work? Church? Some other common interest? When was the last time you told them how special they are to you?

Christmas is the perfect time to reconnect with old friends through letters, phone calls, even email. This little bit of effort is well worth the joy of sharing moments with someone who holds a special place in your heart. Even if you've drifted apart, the pervasive love in this season will guide you back on track.

Appreciate your old friends. Embrace the new. Let the spirit of Christmas—the spirit of shepherds and wise men and angels all gathering to celebrate a special Gift of love—fill your heart with love and compassion.

Friends are angels who lift our feet when
our weary wings have trouble remembering how to fly.

ANONYMOUS

NEW FRIENDS

*T*here's no better time to begin or build a friendship than during the holiday season. It's a time when people are especially inclined to look for the best in each other, when we're more open to the spirit of peace and goodwill. At Christmastime we . . .

Have automatic conversation starters. "What are you doing over the holidays?" "What's your favorite Christmas song?" "I saw a great sale; maybe we could go there together."

Have more opportunities for socializing. Office parties, church parties, neighborhood parties, and the like are constantly cropping up. If you haven't been invited to as many parties as you'd like, throw one yourself. It's a season when that sort of thing is expected.

Make more effort to be charitable. A great way to build a friendship is by partnering with someone to buy gifts for a needy child or family. Or you could volunteer together at a clothing drive or soup kitchen. The opportunities to serve—solo or with others—are endless.

This holiday is truly a season of the heart and spirit, and no heart or spirit was ever meant to live in isolation. We are creatures of relationship. If you see someone who needs a friend, this is a wonderful time to reach out. If you want to make a friend, take advantage of all the holiday opportunities to interact with others. Part of the joy of Christmas is the connection it brings among human beings. Embrace that beautiful gift this year.

Friendship is something that
raises us almost above humanity. . . .
it is the sort of love one
can imagine between angels.

C. S. LEWIS

Joy of a Baby

Behold, the virgin shall be
with child, and bear a Son, and
they shall call His name Immanuel,
which is translated, "God with us."

MATTHEW 2:23

BECAUSE OF A BABY

*O*ne of the best bits of advice I ever received before the birth of my first child was, "If she tells you what she's feeling— good or bad—never ever say to your wife, 'I know just how you feel.'" He was a smart man and I was smart to heed his words of wisdom.

But even as someone of the human species who will never physically experience what it means to bear a child, I still know in my heart that the birth of a baby is one of the most amazing miracles in the world. It's life at its most vital. No matter the pain experienced on the way—and no, I don't know exactly what it feels like—it's clear to see that it's the culmination of innumerable hopes and the beginning of unspeakable joys.

Anyone who knows me well—or even a little—knows that I love everything about Christmas—lights, trees, wreaths, toys, Santa Claus, reindeer, Christmas movies new and old, staring at the night sky, every kind of seasonal music known to humankind, hot chocolate (oh, do I love hot chocolate), frosted sugar cookies (too much), crowds at the mall (call me crazy), entertaining thousands of people in concert venues (hey, it's a tradition for me), and so many other sights and sounds and experiences.

But when I think of Christmas as the season of joy, I can't help but be reminded that two thousand years ago a Baby was born under the most humble of circumstances who brought to us the things that matter the very most—light, life, peace, hope, and love.

Is it any wonder I love Christmas so much?

> *Great little One!*
> *whose all-embracing birth*
> *Lifts Earth to Heaven,*
> *stoops Heaven to Earth.*
>
> RICHARD CRANSHAW

ONE SOLITARY LIFE

BY JAMES FRANCIS

He was born in an obscure village, the child of a peasant woman. He grew up in another village. He worked in a carpenter shop until He was thirty. Then for three years He was an itinerant preacher.

He never owned a home. He never wrote a book. He never held an office. He never had a family. He never went to college. He never put His foot inside a big city. He never traveled two hundred miles from the place He was born. He never did one of the things that usually accompany greatness. He had no credentials but Himself.

While still a young man, the tide of popular opinion turned against him. His friends ran away. One of them denied Him. He was turned over to His enemies. He went through the mockery of a trial. He was nailed upon a cross between two thieves. While He was dying, His executioners gambled for the only piece of property He had on earth—His coat. When He was dead, He was laid in a borrowed grave through the pity of a friend.

Nineteen long centuries have come and gone, and today He is the centerpiece of the human race and leader of the column of progress.

I am far within the mark when I say that all the armies that ever marched, all the navies that were ever built; all the parliaments that ever sat and all the kings that ever reigned, put together, have not affected the life of man upon this earth as powerfully as has that ONE SOLITARY LIFE!

THE CHRISTMAS STORY

LUKE 2:1-20

*A*nd it came to pass in those days that a decree went out from Caesar Augustus that all the world should be registered. . . . So all went to be registered, everyone to his own city.

Joseph also went up from Galilee, out of the city of Nazareth, into Judea, to the city of David, which is called Bethlehem, because he was of the house and lineage of David, to be registered with Mary, his betrothed wife, who was with child. So it was, that while they were there, the days were completed for her to be delivered. And she brought forth her firstborn Son, and wrapped Him in swaddling cloths, and laid Him in a manger, because there was no room for them in the inn. Now there were in the same country shepherds living out in the fields, keeping watch over their flock by night. And behold, an angel of the Lord stood before them, and the glory of the Lord shone around them, and they were greatly afraid. Then the angel said to them, "Do not be afraid, for behold, I bring you good tidings of great joy which will be to all people. For there is born to you this day in the city of David a Savior, who is Christ the Lord. And this will be the sign to you: You will find a Babe wrapped in swaddling cloths, lying in a manger."

And suddenly there was with the angel a multitude of the heavenly host praising God and saying:

"Glory to God in the highest,
And on earth peace, goodwill toward men!"

So it was, when the angels had gone away from them into heaven, that the shepherds said to one another, "Let us now go to Bethlehem and see this thing that has come to pass, which the Lord has made known to us." And they came with haste and found Mary and Joseph, and the Babe lying in a manger. Now when they had seen Him, they made widely known the saying which was told them concerning this Child. And all those who heard it marveled at those things which were told them by the shepherds. But Mary kept all these things and pondered them in her heart. Then the shepherds returned, glorifying and praising God for all the things that they had heard and seen, as it was told them.

You can never truly enjoy Christmas
until you look into the Father's face and tell Him
you have received His Christmas gift.

JOHN R. RICE

Were earth a thousand times as fair
Beset with gold and jewels rare
She yet were far too poor to be
A narrow cradle, Lord, for Thee.

MARTIN LUTHER

Love came down at Christmas,
Love all lovely, Love Divine;
Love was born at Christmas;
Star and angels gave the sign.

CHRISTINA ROSSETTI

To be a joy-bearer and a joy-giver says everything,
for in our life, if one is joyful, it means that one is faithfully living
for God, and that nothing else counts; and if one gives joy
to others, one is doing God's work; with joy without and joy
within, all is well . . . I can think of no higher way.

JANET ERSKINE STUART

God grant you:
The light in Christmas, which is faith.
The warmth in Christmas, which is love.
The radiance of Christmas, which is purity.
The belief in Christmas, which is truth.
The all of Christmas, which is Christ.

WILDA ENGLISH

Make Time for Joy

*L*ately I've been noticing how fast time flies. We recently moved my mom into an assisted living center, and I lost my dad five years ago. Going through my parents' things and seeing knickknacks and plates and coffee mugs I remembered from when I was a child made me realize how quickly life passes.

Joy doesn't just happen. You have to invite it into your life and nurture it in the lives of others. Likewise, Christmas traditions don't just happen; you have to work at fostering the traditions you want for yourself and your family.

Christmas doesn't just happen. Yes, it comes every year on the calendar, but unless you welcome its spirit, then you're going to miss out.

The joy of the Christmas season is what you create. So make time for joy this season. Celebrate the wonder of starry nights and manger scenes; the warmth of memories of family and friends; the joy of music and laughter and being together. Take time to savor this most joyful season of year.

The way you spend Christmas
is far more important
than how much.

HENRY DAVID THOREAU

Christmas is not a time or a season but a state of mind. To
cherish peace and goodwill, to be plenteous in mercy, is to have
the real spirit of Christmas. If we think
on these things, there will be born in us a Savior
and over us all will shine a star, sending
its gleam of hope to the world.

CALVIN COOLIDGE